CONTENTS >>>

2

John Cena is a two-time Royal Rumble winner. He's one of six Superstars (Randy Orton, Hulk Hogan, Shawn Michaels, Stone Cold Steve Austin and Triple H) to win the 30-man match twice.

5

John Cena has won the United States championship a record setting five times.

★ JOHN CENA

16

John Cena is only the second man to be a 16-time World Champion – a first in WWE history. The first man to win 16-Championships, the two-time Hall of Famer, Ric Flair.

1,257

Combined days John Cena has reigned as a WWE Champion—one of the longest reigns in WWE history.

ODD COUPLE

The WWE has seen odd tag teams formed before Sheamus & Cesaro became the mismatched super powers. It can sometimes be a long and bumpy road to forge a perfect pairing to the championship. Can you match these Superstars to their former tag team partner by finding the right road to tag team gold?

Sheamus

Chris Jericho

Goldust

Mankind

Daniel Bryan

Bret Hart

Heath Slater

Rhyno

Goldberg

Booker T

The Miz

The Rock

Cesaro

Kane

Answers on page 76.

RANDY ORTON

HEIGHT: 6'5" **WEIGHT:** 250 pounds
FROM: St. Louis, Missouri
SIGNATURE MOVES: RKO, Middle rope DDT, Superplex

Randy Orton is known as the Apex Predator, but he may now also be the most cerebral Superstar in WWE. Last year he outsmarted and remained fearless when facing and defeating Bray Wyatt. The Viper was also able to secure the WWE Championship, an accomplishment that puts him in the conversation as one of the greatest Superstars in WWE history. The tested veteran continues to surprise the WWE Universe, meaning we could be living through the greatest era of Randy Orton yet.

SAMI ZAYN

HEIGHT: 6'1" **WEIGHT:** 211 pounds
FROM: Quebec, Canada
SIGNATURE MOVES: Helluva Kick, Blue Thunder Bomb, Exploder Suplex

Zayn is easily one of the most popularSuperstars in WWE. The Underdog ofthe Underground is also one of the bravest and most fearless. Whether it's Braun Strowman or his former best bud, Kevin Owens, Zayn will never hesitate to battle in the ring with anyone in WWE and chances are, he'll come up on top. Don't ever give up on Sami, because there is no quit in this exciting Superstar.

AJ STYLES

HEIGHT: 5'11" **WEIGHT:** 218 pounds
FROM: Gainesville, Georgia
SIGNATURE MOVES: Styles Clash, The Phenomenal Forearm, Calf Crusher

The Phenomenal One may have a mean streak, but he's garnered the love and admiration of the WWE Universe. And it's not hard to see why. Styles is one of the most gifted Superstars in WWE history, living up to his moniker as the 'Face Who Runs the Place', Styles has been able to back up everything he's said. He's on a short list of Superstars with a win over John Cena and on an even shorter list of guaranteed future WWE Champions.

SHINSUKE NAKAMURA

HEIGHT: 6'2" **WEIGHT:** 229 pounds
FROM: Kyoto, Japan
SIGNATURE MOVE: Kinshasa

The King of Strong Style is destined for WWE greatness. He already took NXT by storm, becoming a two-time NXT Champion, and his future looks bright on *SmackDown Live*. The charismatic Superstar is known for his unique mannerisms and his captivating entrance, but in the ring, Nakamura is aggressive, unrelenting and a true force to reckon with.

SPOT THE NOT!

We changed ten things on these two awesome images of WWE action. Can you spot all of the slight differences? Prove you're a gold-star member of the WWE Universe by picking every single tiny altered detail on these WWE Superstars.

A

B

Check out the answers on page 76!

CHAMPIONSHIP SCRAMBLE

In the last few years, WWE has undergone a massive championship redesign. Nearly every single piece of gold has been rethought and rebranded to form consistency.

Across the waists and in the arms of your favorite WWE Superstars, the titles are works of art. But up close and at a distorted angle can you tell the difference between every title? It's a tough quiz, but don't worry we offered some hints to help you become the ultimate champion of champions.

Answers on page 76.

1 I'm the most recent title to be introduced to WWE.

2 A WWE Legend took me to my first *WrestleMania* this year.

3 Nearly a dozen WWE Hall of Famers have held me over their shoulder.

4 I've been owned by Bray Wyatt, Macho Man Randy Savage and Edge.

5

I was introduced to the WWE Universe by WWE Hall of Famer, Lita.

6

Alexa Bliss was the first woman to hold me twice.

7

You're looking at the most exciting championship in WWE today.

8

In 2017, we were held by 3 Tag teams, in just six months!

9

We were first held by a team that was dubbed "Beauty and the Man Beast".

10

Seth Rollins, Sami Zayn and Neville all have me in common.

11

No one has held us longer than The Ascension.

12

Believe it or not, but I was never held by Becky Lynch.

13

Chris Jericho and The Miz are my favorite wrestlers.

13

NEW YEAR, NEW RESOLUTIONS

Every new year brings new opportunities for all Superstars. We gathered the best minds on all things WWE to anonymously predict what will happen to Superstars this year.

Sasha Banks

As one of the most popular Superstars in WWE, will next year be the year the WWE Universe sees the bad side of the Boss? Not everyone likes a boss.

John Cena

He always says he'll never give up, but what's left for the 16-time World Champion? After proposing to Nikki Bella at *WrestleMania*, our experts predict that John Cena will step away from the ring for a while, then start seeking his seventeenth title.

AJ Styles

He's arguably the best in all of WWE but after beating John Cena to having the WWE Championship in 2016, what's next for the Phenomenal One? Our experts say this is cloudy, but Styles may be in for his toughest year yet in WWE.

The Miz

He's dominated *SmackDown Live* as the Intercontinental Champion, and our experts say, there'll only be more gold for The Miz. We predict he'll become WWE Champion or Universal Championship before next year's *WrestleMania*.

Shinsuke Nakamura

The King of Strong Style will make *SmackDown Live* his personal playground, and become the most popular Superstar in all of WWE.

James Ellsworth

Our experts predict more will be the same for James Ellsworth. No titles, no wins, no new friends, we don't see much changing for the chinless Superstar.

WHO'S NEXT?

Now's your chance to play fortuneteller: Write down who you think will make these 2018 accomplishments in WWE.

Cesaro

Could this finally be the year when the Swiss Superman wins his first World Championship? Our experts say that this year will be the year when the entire WWE Universe becomes the Cesaro Section.

Becky Lynch

Could the first ever SmackDown Live Women's Champion become the first woman to headline a WWE *SmackDown Live* pay-per-view? We think that's a guarantee.

The Hardys

When Matt & Jeff returned they became Raw Tag Team Champions, so what's left for the greatest team in WWE history? They'll be hard to break-up, but if they went their separate ways, we predict the Hardys will take the WWE Universe to new destinations.

NEXT YEAR, THIS SUPERSTAR WILL DEFINITELY WIN THE UNIVERSAL CHAMPIONSHIP...

NEXT YEAR, THIS SUPERSTAR WILL DEFINITELY WIN THE SMACKDOWN WOMEN'S CHAMPIONSHIP...

NEXT YEAR, THIS SUPERSTAR WILL BECOME WWE CRUISERWEIGHT CHAMPION...

NEXT YEAR, THIS TAG TEAM WILL BREAK UP...

NEXT YEAR, THIS SUPERSTAR WILL LEAVE NXT AND JOIN EITHER RAW OR SMACKDOWN LIVE...

NEXT YEAR, VINCE MCMAHON WILL MAKE THIS PERSON THE GM OF *RAW*...

NEXT YEAR, THIS SUPERSTAR WILL DEFINITELY WIN THE WWE CHAMPIONSHIP...

NEXT YEAR, VINCE MCMAHON WILL MAKE THIS PERSON THE GM OF *SMACKDOWN LIVE*...

NEXT YEAR, THIS SUPERSTAR WILL DEFINITELY WIN THE *RAW* WOMEN'S CHAMPIONSHIP...

NEXT YEAR, THIS SUPERSTAR WILL HEADLINE *WRESTLEMANIA*...

NEXT YEAR, THIS WWE LEGEND WILL BECOME A WWE HALL OF FAMER...

2018 WILL BE A BREAKOUT YEAR FOR...

THE BIG QUIZ
TEST YOUR MIGHT!

ARE YOU THE MOST KNOWLEDGEABLE MEMBER OF THE WWE UNIVERSE? THIS QUIZ WILL SEPARATE THE CASUAL FANS FROM THE WWE FAITHFUL.

Q.1
WHAT WAS THE FIRST MATCH ON THE FIRST RAW OF 2017?

A Seth Rollins vs. Kevin Owens

B Bayley vs. Nia Jax

C Xavier Woods vs. Titus O'Neil

Q.2
WHAT WAS THE MAIN EVENT OF THE FIRST *SMACKDOWN LIVE* OF 2017?

A Becky Lynch vs. La Luchadora

B American Alpha vs. Breezango

C Baron Corbin vs. Dolph Ziggler

Q.3
WHAT MATCH DID CHRIS JERICHO INVENT?

A Elimination Chamber

B Money in the Bank

C Ambrose Asylum

Q.4
WHAT TYPE OF MATCH HAVE RANDY ORTON AND JOHN CENA NOT HAD?

A TLC Match

B I Quit Match

C Strap Match

Q.5
WHICH OF THESE SUPERSTARS NEVER WON A MONEY IN THE BANK?

A Big Show

B Big Poppa Pump

C Big Gene Snitsky

Q.6
WHICH OF THESE EVENTS IS NOT A WWE PAY-PER-VIEW?

A *Badd Blood*

B *Backlash*

C *Thunder*

Q.7
KANE HAS WON TAG TEAM GOLD WITH ANYONE EXCEPT...

A X-Pac

B Daniel Bryan

C Dolph Ziggler

Q.8
WHERE IS BIG CASS FROM?

A Queens, New York

B Boston, Massachusetts

C Daytona, Florida

Q.9
WHO WAS THE FIRST EVER 2-TIME NXT CHAMPION?

A	Seth Rollins	
B	Sami Zayn	
C	Samoa Joe	

Q.10
WHICH OF THESE WWE SUPERSTARS' FATHERS IS NOT A WWE LEGEND?

A	Natalya	
B	The Usos	
C	Chad Gable	

Q.11
PICK THE CHAMPIONSHIP ROMAN REIGNS HAS YET TO WIN.

A	Intercontinental Championship	
B	U.S. Championship	
C	WWE Championship	

Q.12
WHO IS NOT OFFICIALLY NAMED "BIG"?

A	Big Show	
B	Big Poppa Pump	
C	Big Gene Snitsky	

Q.13
WHO DID MR. McMAHON DEFEAT TO WIN THE WWE CHAMPIONSHIP?

A	Triple H	
B	The Rock	
C	Stone Cold	

Q.14
WHO DID JEFF HARDY DEFEAT TO WIN HIS FIRST WWE CHAMPIONSHIP IN A TRIPLE THREAT MATCH?

A	Matt Hardy & Christian	
B	Edge & Triple H	
C	Randy Orton & Kurt Angle	

Q.15
IN HIS WWE DEBUT MATCH, WHO DID FANDANGO DEFEAT?

A	Tyler Breeze	
B	Chris Jericho	
C	Dolph Ziggler	

Q.16
WHICH WWE SUPERSTAR WAS NOT IN 'SCOOBY-DOO! *WRESTLEMANIA* MYSTERY'?

A	John Cena	
B	Charlotte	
C	Vince McMahon	

Q.17
WHICH SUPERSTAR'S ENTRANCE MUSIC HAS THE LYRICS, 'THEY BROKE THE MOLD, WHEN THEY MADE ME'?

A	Tyler Breeze	
B	Dolph Ziggler	
C	Sasha Banks	

Q.18
WHICH OF THESE SUPERSTARS WAS NEVER A WWE WOMEN'S CHAMPION?

A	Stephanie McMahon	
B	Alicia Fox	
C	Summer Rae	

Q.19
WHICH OF THESE SUPERSTARS HAS NOT WRESTLED BAREFOOT?

A	Rusev	
B	The Bushwhackers	
C	Jimmy Snuka	

Q.20
WHAT IS THE NAME OF SHINSUKE NAKAMURA'S THEME SONG?

A	The Rising Sun	
B	Kinshasa	
C	The King of Strong Style	

AWESOME JOB! CHECK YOUR ANSWERS ON PAGE 76!

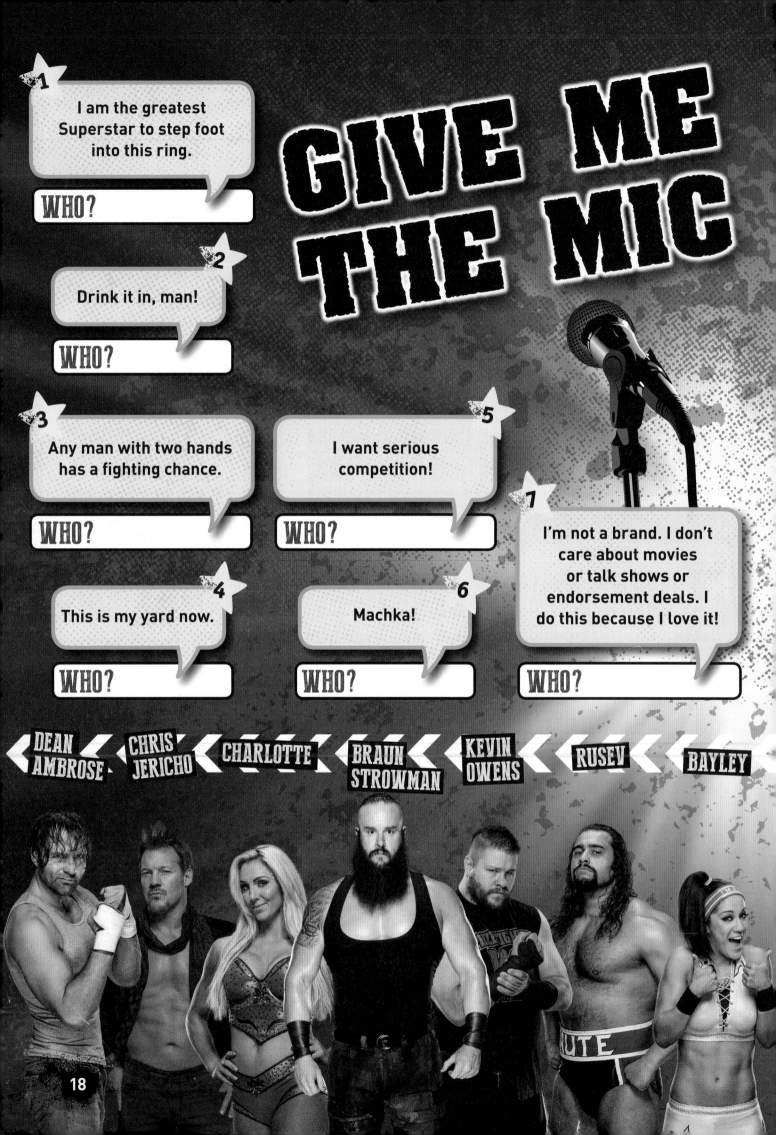

GIVE ME THE MIC

1

I am the greatest Superstar to step foot into this ring.

WHO?

2

Drink it in, man!

WHO?

3

Any man with two hands has a fighting chance.

WHO?

5

I want serious competition!

WHO?

4

This is my yard now.

WHO?

6

Machka!

WHO?

7

I'm not a brand. I don't care about movies or talk shows or endorsement deals. I do this because I love it!

WHO?

DEAN AMBROSE   CHRIS JERICHO   CHARLOTTE   BRAUN STROWMAN   KEVIN OWENS   RUSEV   BAYLEY

The only thing worse than receiving a Superstar's finisher is the verbal smack that comes before it. Here are 14 random Superstar quotes, but they're not all catchphrases. Can you match the words of war to its originator?

12
I'm back taking souls and digging holes!

WHO?

8
They don't get booty, they stay booty!

WHO?

10
I look the part, I act the part, I walk the part, I talk the part, because I am the part.

WHO?

13
The 12-year-old in my heart wouldn't have had her *WrestleMania* moment come true if it wasn't for you guys."

WHO?

9
I am the new face of America.

WHO?

11
I am the reaper. What makes you think that you are immune to me?

WHO?

14
You never know what, or who's next.

WHO?

Answers on page 76.

ROMAN REIGNS ◄ THE MIZ ◄ UNDERTAKER GOLDBERG ◄ JAMES ELLSWORTH ◄◄ THE NEW DAY ◄ ◄

FINN BÁLOR

HEIGHT: 5'11" **WEIGHT:** 190 pounds
FROM: Bray, County Wicklow, Ireland
SIGNATURE MOVES: Coup de Grâce, Sling Blade

In a short amount of time, Finn Bálor has shown the WWE Universe an incredible range in character and in his in-ring arsenal. Since his return to *Raw* the night after *WrestleMania*, Bálor has surged as a top contender for the Universal Championship. And then there's The Demon King. The painted mysterious alter ego of Bálor is only unleashed to bring a deeper, darker side putting a stop to all who stand against him. Don't be surprised when the Demon rules Monday nights.

THE MIZ

HEIGHT: 6'2" **WEIGHT:** 221 pounds
FROM: Cleveland, Ohio
SIGNATURE MOVES: Skull Crushing Finale, Awesome Clothesline, Figure-Four Leg Lock

There isn't anyone else in WWE who's more hated and more full of himself than The Miz. The self-proclaimed A-Lister, and his wife Maryse, set *SmackDown Live* on fire with his scalding words against John Cena, Dolph Ziggler and even the GM, Daniel Bryan. On *Raw*, not much has changed. Considering The Miz's fiery path, he may just be as good as he says he is.

CHRIS JERICHO

HEIGHT: 6'0" **WEIGHT:** 227 pounds
FROM: Winnipeg, Manitoba, Canada
SIGNATURE MOVES: Walls of Jericho, Codebreaker, Lionsault

The veteran of the *Raw* locker room, Chris Jericho has completed feats in WWE that most Superstars will never achieve. Despite his various accomplishments, The G.O.A.T. has yet to capture the WWE Universal Title. Now that his rivalry with Kevin Owens is in the dust, maybe it's time for Y2J to rule *Raw* once again and transform it back to Monday Night Jericho. It wouldn't be too hard to drink that in, maaaaaan!

BRAUN STROWMAN

HEIGHT: 6'8" **WEIGHT:** 385 pounds
FROM: Sherrills Ford, North Carolina
SIGNATURE MOVE: Running Powerslam

BRAAAAAAAUN! When the WWE Universe hears that, they know whoever is facing the Monster Among Men will obliterate whatever is in front of him. Braun Strowman is single handedly the most destructive force in WWE today. There are no signs of him slowing down and Strowman is still at the start of a young career. And those who stand in his way are all but guaranteed an even shorter career.

KINGDOM OF KINGS

THE BITES OF THE BRITISH BULLDOGS

The historic tag team of Davey Boy Smith and the Dynamite Kid were two of the earliest Superstars to bring British style wrestling to the worldwide reach of WWE. They had classic matches against the Hart Foundation and won the Tag Team Championships.

THE WWE EUROPEAN CHAMPIONSHIP

In 1997 WWE launched a tournament to crown their first ever European Champion. The winner was WWE Legend The British Bulldog, who was also the longest reigning champ. And in just five short years, the title went on to be held by the likes of Triple H, Christian, Matt Hardy, Chris Jericho, and WWE Hall of Famers Shawn Michaels, Kurt Angle, Eddie Guerrero and Diamond Dallas Page.

BRITISH BULLDOG*

1984

1992

1997

1998

SUMMERSLAM IN LONDON

The first and only WWE pay-per-view held outside of North America was arguably the biggest *SummerSlam* ever. Over 80,000 members of the WWE Universe jam-packed Wembley Stadium to see "Macho Man" Randy Savage battle the Ultimate Warrior. The main event was Bret "Hit Man" Hart taking on The British Bulldog in an unbelievable classic bout.

WILLIAM REGAL PUNCHES IN

All hail the king! William Regal is one of the most respected WWE Legends from overseas. The General Manager of NXT was a key authority in the Cruiserweight Classic and the UK Division. Regal has done everything there is to do in WWE, and may be considered the greatest British born Superstar in WWE history. A former Intercontinental Champion, European Champion, Tag Team Champion, and King of the Ring winner, Regal was known for his underhanded tactics such as using brass knuckles and his deadly submissions. Regal has a lighter side too. He's had some funny moments in WWE, but he's still one of the toughest and one of the greatest.

The WWE's United Kingdom division is not the first time WWE has explored the UK. WWE has a rich history with the united countries. Here are some of WWE's most memorable moments with all things United Kingdom.

NEVILLE FLIES IN

The high-flying, gravity defying Superstar, Neville, is unlike most. With a deep arsenal, Neville has captured the NXT Championship and set a firm grasp on the Cruiserweight Title. Neville, despite his attitude change is an amazing Superstar to watch, and hopefully will make UK fans proud of his amazing accomplishments.

TYLER BATE AND THE UNITED KINGDOM CHAMPIONSHIP

In the two-night tournament, Tyler Bate became the first ever United Kingdom Champion. Sixteen men battled for the beautiful and prestigious title in hard striking contests. In the end, Bate, from Dudley, England, was able to best Pete Dunne in the final. So far, the United Kingdom Champion has had a few title defenses on WWE TV, including one hard fought battle against Cruiserweight contender, Jack Gallagher. But after witnessing the incredible UK Tournament, there's a lot of promise surrounding the young division, and a big sign of the global expansion for WWE.

2009

2013

2014

2016

BROGUE KICK START

The Celtic Warrior made an impactful WWE debut on ECW. In less than six months, the pale warrior went on to become WWE Champion by defeating John Cena. Since then Sheamus has gone on to have a decorated resume. The Great White has won the World Championship, United States Title, the King of the Ring crown, Royal Rumble and Money in the Bank. Sheamus is arguably one of the best UK born Superstars of all time and he continues to dominate in the ring, whether he's teaming up with Cesaro or just delivering a Brogue Kick to whoever is standing in his way.

ENTER THE LASS KICKER

Becky Lynch made her debut in WWE in early 2014 in NXT. From there, Lynch has gone on to make WWE history. As part of the Women's Revolution, Lynch stole the show at *WrestleMania 32* facing Sasha Banks and Charlotte. Lynch is WWE's first Irish born women's competitor and is bound for greatness no matter what continent she's on.

BECKY LYNCH

HEIGHT: 5'6"
FROM: Dublin, Ireland
SIGNATURE MOVES: Bex-plex, Dis-arm-her,
Four Leg Clover

The first ever SmackDown Women's Champion is looking to regain her footing on Tuesday nights. Becky Lynch has been explosive since joining Team Blue, but the competitive women's division has kept Lynch away from gold. And we're guessing that will not be the case for long. Lynch has big Superstar dreams and no one will prevent her from making Tuesday nights straight fire!

CHARLOTTE FLAIR

HEIGHT: 5'10"
FROM: The Queen City
SIGNATURE MOVES: Figure-Eight Leg Lock,
Bow Down to the Queen

The Queen of WWE has moved to *SmackDown Live* after dominating *Raw* for months and it's hard to not imagine her ruling the show. The Genetically Superior Athlete has shown so many trademarks of her father: arrogant, brash, and incredibly talented in the ring. At this rate Charlotte is on her way to becoming one of the greatest Superstars in WWE history, period.

ALEXA BLISS

HEIGHT: 5'0"
FROM: Columbus, Ohio
SIGNATURE MOVE: Twisted Bliss

Alexa Bliss has come a long way in a short time in WWE. Already a two-time WWE SmackDown Women's Champion, Bliss, now on *Raw*, is looking to permanently keep the women's division spotlight squarely on her. Whether it's Mickie James, Sasha Banks or even Nia Jax, Bliss will do whatever it takes to make sure she's the only *Raw* Superstar on your mind.

BAYLEY

HEIGHT: 5'6"
FROM: San Jose, California
SIGNATURE MOVES: Bayley-to-Belly Suplex, Top rope elbow

High fives! Bayley is one of the most infectious Superstars today. Her bubbly personality and her hug life motto makes her so much fun to watch. A lifelong member of the WWE Universe, Bayley is living proof that anyone can achieve their dreams of becoming a champion in WWE.

FANTASY WARFARE

BROCK LESNAR

SURVIVOR SERIES

Brock Lesnar vs. Goldberg was a dream rematch no one thought could happen again. At Survivor Series 2016, Goldberg returned from retirement to have one last dream match up, and to everyone's surprise, he defeated Brock Lesnar in less than two minutes.

That only infuriated the Beast.

20 years ago, Goldberg was a historic and destructive champion in WCW. He was just as tough when he joined WWE in 2003. At *WrestleMania XX*, Lesnar and Goldberg faced off for the first time, igniting this long time rivalry, and on that night, Goldberg won.

WRESTLEMANIA XX

How the biggest dream match in WWE history became one of the biggest rivalries for the Universal Championship at *WrestleMania*.

GOLDBERG

In the last 5 years, The Beast became more powerful than anyone could imagine. He conquered the UFC, destroyed John Cena, and crushed Undertaker's *WrestleMania* streak. When Goldberg returned to WWE as an exclusive part of the new WWE video game in 2016, the rumors started: what if he returned to the ring?

Goldberg, after a decade away from the ring, came back, crushed Lesnar and won the Universal Championship. In the biggest rematch at *WrestleMania* these two titans clashed for the final time.

BROCK LESNAR
VS
GOLDBERG

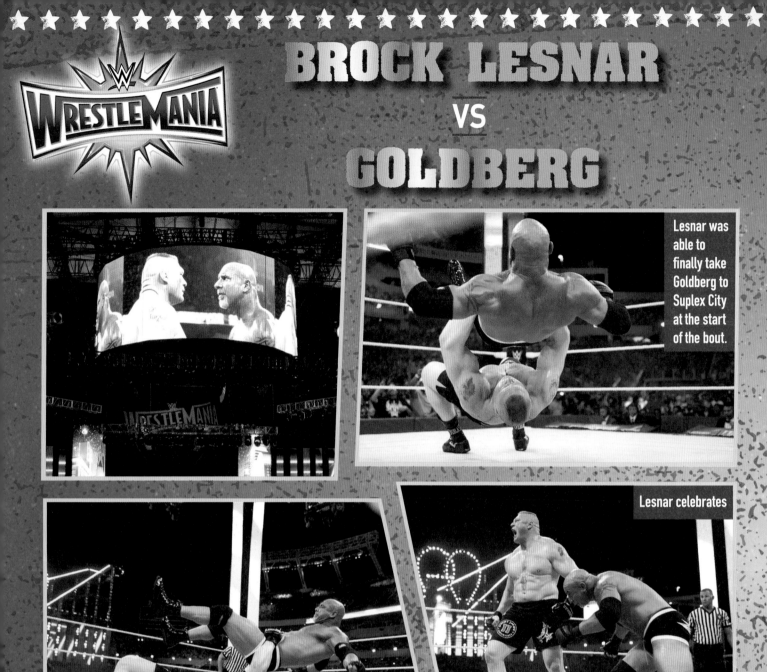

Lesnar was able to finally take Goldberg to Suplex City at the start of the bout.

Lesnar celebrates

But Goldberg immediately fired back with a Spear!

Then another Spear!

And then Speared Lesnar through the outside barricade!

Goldberg was able to follow through with another Spear and a Jack Hammer but Lesnar kicked out.

To Goldberg's surprise, Lesnar dodged another Spear with a super human leapfrog.

Then it was time to re-enter Suplex City: 10 German suplexes was the prelude:

With an F5 for the victory.

By the end of *WrestleMania*, Brock was back, and back on top of Raw.

ROMAN REIGNS VS UNDERTAKER

In a No Holds Barred Match, Roman Reigns battled Undertaker in a war to be the top dog in the yard. For the first time ever, these two Superstars faced each other and the result was one of the most emotional moments in WWE history.

The two biggest dogs in WWE finally collided in a hard-hitting fight.

It didn't take long for the battle to move outside of the ring.

Undertaker proved he still had what it takes to run the WWE yard, countering most of Reigns' arsenal, including the Drive-By.

He Choke Slammed Roman on a table...

Of course, Reigns and his incredible toughness took Undertaker down with a Spear and through a table.

Reigns took the fight to Undertaker, delivering punches to Undertaker in the corner.

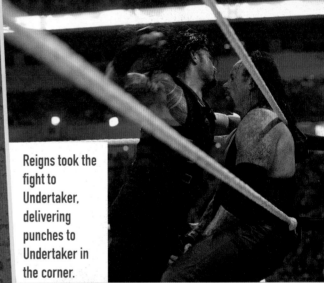

But Undertaker countered with his deep arsenal and dished out the Last Ride.

Reigns kicked out and the Dead Man upped the stakes and got a steel chair.

After a series of chair shots, Reigns delivered three Superman punches to Undertaker. On the fourth attempt. . .

The Phenom countered with a choke slam on the steel chair.

Then came a Tombstone.

Roman Reigns kicked out!

The momentum swung into the Roman Empire's direction as he delivered a Superman Punch and a Spear, but Undertaker countered again with the Hell's Gate.

Roman was able to get a break when he reached the ropes.

As Undertaker crawled to the steel chair, Roman got there first and delivered chair shots to the Dead Man's back.

Roman followed with a Spear, and Undertaker surprisingly kicked out!

Another Spear. And another kick out!

Roman didn't back down and after hitting the ropes, he delivered the final Spear to defeat the Undertaker.

Roman's biggest victory in his career also makes him only the second man to defeat Undertaker at *WrestleMania*.

Roman didn't look like he wanted to topple Undertaker, but he proved once and for all that it's his yard.

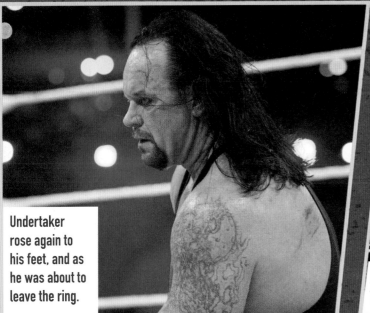

Undertaker rose again to his feet, and as he was about to leave the ring.

As the WWE Universe showed with their love with "Thank you, Taker" cheers, the Undertaker returned to the center of the ring.

He removed the gloves from his hands, removed his entrance jacket and for the last time, he removed his hat.

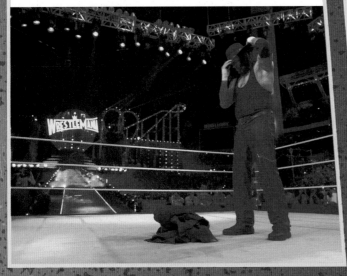

The gear stayed in the center of the ring, a symbolic gesture by the Dead Man.

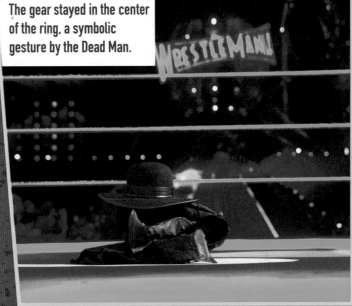

As he walked up the ramp, Undertaker made, what many believe to be, his final appearance in WWE.

One of the greatest Superstars in WWE history said goodbye in his way, and if this is goodbye, then thank you, Taker.

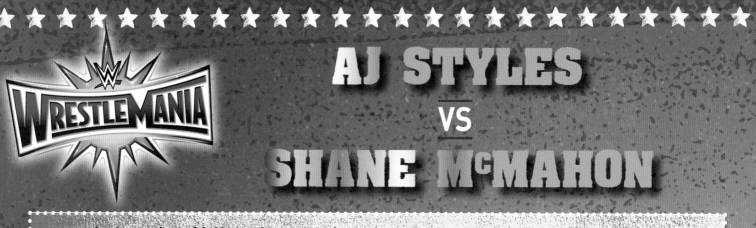

AJ STYLES
VS
SHANE McMAHON

In the real world, if you threw your boss through a car window that would certainly lead to an appearance in court and a search for a new job, In WWE, it just leads to a *WrestleMania* moment. The first official match of *WrestleMania 33* saw AJ Styles take on his boss, the commissioner of *SmackDown Live*, Shane McMahon.

From the get go, Styles was trash talking in the ring about how he was going to embarrass McMahon.

Styles, certainly had a lead, delivering a baseball slide to send Shane up and over the ringside announce table.

It didn't take Shane O Mac long to get the upper hand.

He is the man who went toe-to-toe with Undertaker last year in Hell in a Cell, so you should never count out Shane.

He countered AJ's highflying arsenal early in the bout.

And Shane continued with a flurry of punches and a spinning back elbow, and even an Angle Slam — an homage to WWE Hall of Famer and his former rival, Kurt Angle.

Styles swung the momentum in his favor putting Shane in the dreaded Calf Crusher submission.

Shane, however, reversed the hold to his own submission.

Shane was also able to counter the 450 Splash, by catching Styles in midair, for another submission. But being the Phenomenal One, Styles countered the submission with the Styles Clash. But Shane kicked out.

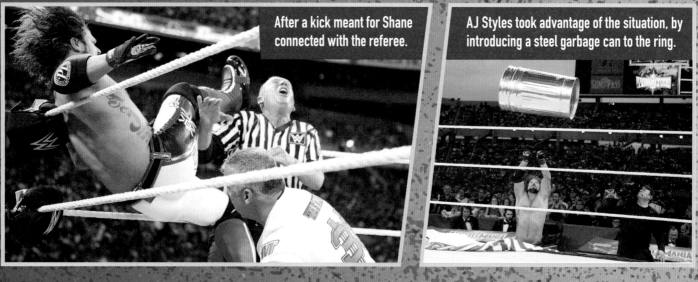

After a kick meant for Shane connected with the referee.

AJ Styles took advantage of the situation, by introducing a steel garbage can to the ring.

Taking a page from Shane's book, Styles went for the Coast-to-Coast but Shane countered with a trashcan to the face of Styles in midair!

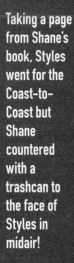

So Shane decided to dish out his signature move: the Coast-to-Coast.

1...2...KICK OUT! Styles kicked out!

Shane then went to ready the announcer's table.

He went for the leaping elbow drop to the outside of the ring, but Styles dodged a disaster.

After Styles missed with the Phenomenal Forearm...

Shane went for a Shooting Star Press ... And missed!

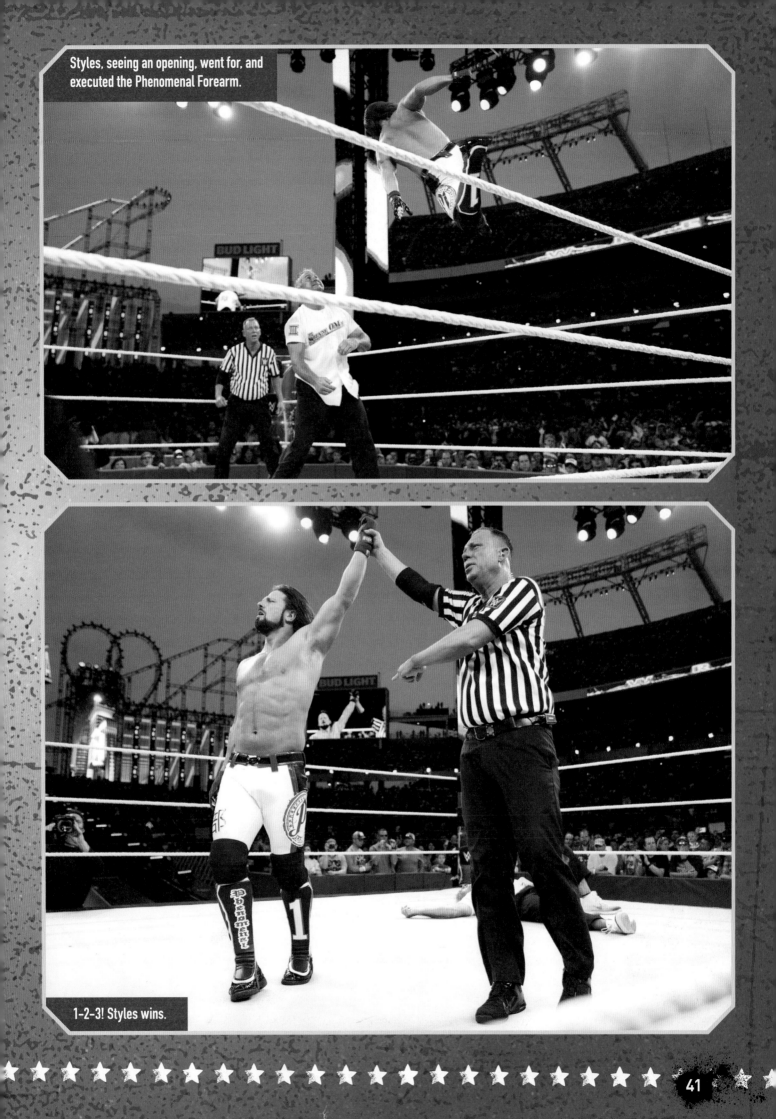

Styles, seeing an opening, went for, and executed the Phenomenal Forearm.

1-2-3! Styles wins.

WrestleMania 33 was the biggest, most exciting and the most stacked 'Mania in history. The show clocked in at more than five hours long, so we decided to highlight the biggest moments in the star-studded show including the shocking return of the Hardys, Seth Rollins' amazing one-legged battle against Triple H, Randy Orton's cerebral war with Bray Wyatt and the fallout of the SmackDown Women's Championship Match.

HIGHLIGHTS

EXTREME COMEBACK

Matt and Jeff, the Hardys made a shocking, exciting comeback to WWE, by entering the Raw Tag Team Ladder Match between Enzo & Cass, Sheamus & Cesaro and the champs, The Club.

The Hardys jaw-dropping, hair raising return turned Camping World Stadium on its toes and used their ladder expertise and their shocking comeback to take advantage of their surprised opponents. Jeff's daredevil ways took out Cesaro and Sheamus with a Swanton Bomb off a ladder, while Matt climbed a ladder inside the ring to win their seventh WWE Tag Team Championships.

The Hardys are finally back in WWE and they are immediately back on top of the WWE Tag Team Division.

MANIA MADNESS

In his 13th WrestleMania, Randy Orton defeated Bray Wyatt to win his 13th WWE Championship. This sick and twisted rivalry was filled with more turns and twists than a roller coaster, as Orton joined the Wyatt Family, helped Bray win the WWE Championship only to betray the Eater of Worlds. No one has ever been able to match Wyatt in mind games, until the Apex Predator.

The match itself saw some bizarre moments by Bray. The buzzard leader somehow was able to project disturbing visuals onto the ring, but in the end, Randy Orton proved nothing is stronger than an RKO. From outta nowhere, Orton finally toppled his former leader, winning his historic 13th World Championship.

The rivalry was far from over, but for the moment, Orton was able to prove that Wyatt's mind games had no effect on the veteran Superstar.

SIX-PACK CHAOS

For the first time ever, the SmackDown Women's Championship was defended at *WrestleMania*. Alex Bliss entered the bout as Champion and the odds were stacked against her. Becky Lynch, Natalya, Carmella, Naomi and Mickie James battled for supremacy. Even James Ellsworth received a Bex-plex for his troubles. In the end, Naomi was able to make Bliss tap out to win her second SmackDown Women's Championship in front of her hometown crowd of Orlando.

FATAL FURY

In her first ever *WrestleMania*, Bayley entered the ring as the Raw Women's Champion. With the WWE Universe firmly behind the Champion, Bayley needed every advantage to topple the three other women against her: Charlotte, Nia Jax and Sasha Banks. Bayley overcame the odds and outlasted the other three women to retain her championship.

THE KING IS DEAD. LONG LIVE THE KING!

Seth Rollins earned his new nickname as King Slayer, defeating Triple H in an Unsanctioned Match. It was a long, winding rivalry between the two. The King of Kings cost Seth Rollins the WWE Universal Championship and after a brutal sneak attack by Samoa Joe, Triple H nearly ended The Architect's career.

Seth Rollins, with a bad, surgically repaired right knee, somehow managed to defeat Triple H with a Pedigree at *WrestleMania*. Rollins' herculean, one-legged effort not only gave him some long overdue revenge, but he put the cherry on top by sending Triple H into Stephanie McMahon who went through a table!

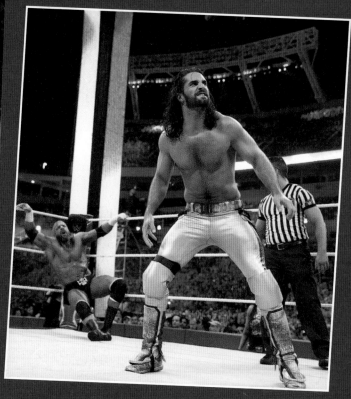

We don't know what's next for Rollins, but with Triple H behind him, now Rollins can finally focus on *Raw's* biggest prize: the Universal Championship.

THE HARDYS

MATT HARDY
HEIGHT: 6'2"
WEIGHT: 236 pounds
FROM: Cameron, North Carolina
SIGNATURE MOVES: Twist of Fate, Swanton Bomb, Poetry in Motion,

JEFF HARDY
HEIGHT: 6'1"
WEIGHT: 225 pounds

The Hardys sent the WWE Universe into complete shock when they made their surprising return at *WrestleMania* and captured the *Raw* Tag Team titles. It's been years since Matt and Jeff were in a WWE ring together and their time away has only made fans miss their death defying thirst for high risk. As in-ring veterans, you can only imagine what the Hardys will do next to secure their footing as one the greatest teams, but also two of the greatest Superstars ever.

ENZO & BIG CASS

ENZO AMORE
HEIGHT: 5'11"
WEIGHT: 200 pounds
FROM: Hackensack, New Jersey
SIGNATURE MOVE: Bada Boom Shakalaka

BIG CASS
HEIGHT: 7'0"
WEIGHT: 276 pounds
FROM: Queens, New York

Bada boom! These are the realest guys in the room! The *Raw* tag team is blessed with the gift of gab. Plus, Enzo's unique looks and Cass's power makes them a classic throwback team. Enzo and Cass have yet to win WWE tag team gold (and that includes *NXT*), but when they do, we're sure the entire WWE Universe will be screaming, "How you doin'!"

AMERICAN ALPHA

CHAD GABLE
HEIGHT: 5'8"
WEIGHT: 203 pounds
FROM: Minneapolis, Minnesota

JASON JORDAN
HEIGHT: 6'3"
WEIGHT: 245 pounds
FROM: Chicago, Illnois

SIGNATURE MOVES: Grand Amplitude, Tech Fall

These two incredibly gifted young Superstars are known for their high velocity, high impact moves in WWE. It's easy to root for American Alpha because they're exciting to watch and their intensity rubs off on the WWE Universe. With one of the strongest team finishers in WWE, it won't be long until Alpha starts making tag team history.

THE NEW DAY

KOFI KINGSTON
HEIGHT: 6'0"
WEIGHT: 212 pounds
FROM: Ghana, West Africa

BIG E
HEIGHT: 5'11"
WEIGHT: 285 pounds
FROM: Tampa, Florida

XAVIER WOODS
HEIGHT: 5'11"
WEIGHT: 205 pounds
FROM: Atlanta, Georgia

SIGNATURE MOVES: Midnight Hour, Unicorn Stampede

Arguably the greatest tag team in modern WWE history, the New Day has exceeded all expectations since their debut to become a history-making trio. Whether it's unicorn horns, Booty-O's cereal or New Day ice cream, Big E, Woods and Kingston are three of the most entertaining Superstars in all WWE. In the ring, they're a well-balanced unit that other teams could learn from. They could be one team on a short list who never separate, craving a new path in tag team wrestling and that's exciting. Because... New. Day. Rocks!

As part of the 2018 WWE Annual launch Delzinski, Little Brother Books & WWE Games teamed up to run a competition to create a Superstar in *WWE 2K17* with the winning creation being featured in this years WWE Annual.

After many awesome Superstars were submitted via the *WWE 2K17* Playstation 4 Community Creations Suite using the hashtag #LBBAnnual, one Superstar was chosen!

That Superstar was Aperel Anubis created by Matthew Chapman from North Shields, UK.

★ ★ Congratulations on winning the #LBBAnnual Competition.

CREATED SUPERSTAR STATS

NAME: Aperel Anubis

HEIGHT: 6'0"

WEIGHT: 202 lbs

FROM (location): Giza, Egypt

SIGNATURE MOVE (finisher): Flip Piledriver

DID YOU KNOW? (a cool fact about Anubis):

Aperel Anubis's name and look is based on the ancient Egyptian God of the dead.

A little bit about your creation and what made you create him in the way that you did:

When I was helping my little brother with homework about ancient Egypt, I started to look at the Gods they worshipped in those times. Out of all of them I thought that Anubis looked the best for a wrestler. I wanted him to have a very Egyptian look, so when people looked at him visually they could tell that he was inspired by Ancient Egypt.

Favourite Superstar or Rival Super which you would have Anubis perform his finisher on:

I would like his rival to be Chris Jericho one of my favourite heels of all time, I would like to see Aperel Anubis perform his finisher on him.

DELZINSKI >>>

YouTube Channel:
www.youtube.com/vintageshizzle

Website: www.delzinski.com

Twitter: @Delzinski

Instagram: @Delzinski

Delzinski is a WWE Gamer and Wrestling Enthusiast who runs a popular YouTube channel with over 70,000 Subscribers and 20 Million video views. The channel content includes concepts for future WWE Games, Epic Simulations and his highly popular Universe Mode where Delzinski controls the WWE Universe which is every fans dream!

Delzinski has worked with 2K UK over the last few years supporting the WWE 2K Franchise which has given him the opportunity to meet and interview WWE Superstars such as Big Show, Finn Balor, The New Day and Goldberg. Delzinski's content has also caught the eye of COO Triple H with his United Kingdom Championship creation being featured on WWE.com

Did you know? Delzinski's favourite Superstar is the ICON Sting!

You can check out Delzinski's content by using the links above.

49

THE BIG QUIZ
FACT OR FICTION?

TRUE OR FALSE? THIS QUIZ WILL BE A FUN GAME OF WITS FOR ALL MEMBERS OF THE WWE UNIVERSE. CAN YOU SPOT THE TRUTHS FROM THE LEGENDS?

1 Chris Jericho has never won the *Royal Rumble* match.

TRUE ☐ FALSE ☐

2 Finn Bálor is the longest reigning Universal Champion in WWE history.

TRUE ☐ FALSE ☐

3 John Cena is a former Intercontinental Champion.

TRUE ☐ FALSE ☐

4 The United States Championship has never changed hands at *WrestleMania*.

TRUE ☐ FALSE ☐

5 Big E is a former United States Champion.

TRUE ☐ FALSE ☐

6 The Rock has never won the WWE Championship at *WrestleMania*.

TRUE ☐ FALSE ☐

7 Sheamus is undefeated in Tables Matches.

TRUE ☐ FALSE ☐

8 Gallows & Anderson were never in NXT.

TRUE ☐ FALSE ☐

50

9 Goldust had a match at *WrestleMania XII*.

TRUE ☐   FALSE ☐

10 Curt Hawkins and Zack Ryder are a former tag team.

TRUE ☐   FALSE ☐

11 Mark Henry faced the Undertaker in a Buried Alive Match at *WrestleMania 22*.

TRUE ☐   FALSE ☐

12 The Brian Kendrick is one of the longest reigning Tag Team Champions in WWE history.

TRUE ☐   FALSE ☐

13 WWE Hall of Famer Booker T is a former announcer for NXT.

TRUE ☐   FALSE ☐

14 The Bellas are former SmackDown Tag Team Champions.

TRUE ☐   FALSE ☐

15 Maryse is a former two-time WWE Divas Champion.

TRUE ☐   FALSE ☐

16 There have been more *Survivor Series* events than *Summer Slam* events.

TRUE ☐   FALSE ☐

17 Curtis Axel is the son of WWE Hall of Famer, Mr. Perfect.

TRUE ☐   FALSE ☐

18 Braun Strowman was once in the Wyatt Family.

TRUE ☐   FALSE ☐

19 Daniel Bryan defeated Chris Jericho in his WWE debut match.

TRUE ☐   FALSE ☐

20 Heath Slater is a four-time Tag Team Champion.

TRUE ☐   FALSE ☐

WWE 205

If you're not watching the Cruiserweights on WWE's weekly series, *205 Live*, you're missing rollercoaster like excitement. Here are 5 reasons why *205 Live* is WWE's most exciting hour on TV.

HIGH RISK, HIGH REWARD

1 *205 Live* is the only place where every Superstar is skilled in high flying, high risk and posseses a high-octane arsenal. With all due respect with the rest of the WWE roster, the Cruiserweights offer the most jaw-dropping excitement from bell-to-bell.

EXCLUSIVE TO *RAW*

2 The WWE Cruiserweights have their own show with 205 Live, but they're also exclusive to *Monday Night Raw*. Where else can you get a double dose of your favorite Superstars in just one week?

AUSTIN ARIES' RETURN

3 After sitting at the announce table with entertaining insight and a skewed expertise, Austin Aries fully healed from an injury and returned to WWE. Aries went straight to the top – attacking Neville – on the March 7 episode of *205 Live*. The confrontation lead to a classic bout between the two at *WrestleMania*, with Neville winning, the exciting Aries can now battle a new crop of Cruiserweight contenders.

GENTLEMAN DUELS

4 Not all of the action is in the ring on *205 Live* – especially when Jack Gallagher is involved. The Extraordinary Gentleman is unlike past WWE Superstars. Instead of loud trash talk, Gallagher would rather use his umbrella "William III" to outsmart a Superstar. He'll even use to help his aerial arsenal in the ring.

THE CRUISERWEIGHT CLASSIC

5 *205 Live* was launched through the breathtaking WWE tournament, the Cruiserweight Classic. Available only on the WWE Network, the tourney saw 32 Superstars, both new and old compete to become the first ever WWE Cruiserweight Champion. Watch it. It's amazing.

When Stephanie McMahon ushered the Women's Revolution to WWE, Becky Lynch debuted with Charlotte and Sasha Banks as they shook up the Women's Division on *Monday Night Raw*. It was not too long after her debut that Lynch teamed up with Paige and Charlotte to form Team PCB. The trio took on Team B.A.D. and Team Bella. Eventually the group imploded and the Superstars started to crave their own path.

Although she debuted as Becky Lynch in NXT, the Lass Kicker that we know today wasn't quite there yet. Still, Lynch was firecracker of a Superstar with big ambitions and took on other NXT Superstars like Sasha Banks and Summer Rae.

As Lynch started to rack up the wins, her character started to change and so did her attire. The green gear was gone and the orange haired Lass Kicker was born. Lynch added some goggles and a top hat and the Lynch you know today was at *NXT Takeover* in August 2015 and took on Charlotte, Emma, and Dana Brooke in a Women's Fatal 4-Way.

WWE DEBUT

THEN, NOW, FOREVER

So many of today's Superstars get their big WWE break in NXT, including SmackDown Live's Becky Lynch. Relive the evolution of The Lass Kicker from her start at NXT to becoming SmackDown's first Women's Champion.

At their 'Mania debut, Lynch, Charlotte, and Sasha Banks stole the show competing for the newly minted WWE Women's Championship. The three Superstars put on a performance of a lifetime. And although it was Charlotte who won the match, Lynch had cemented her foundation as one of the best in WWE today.

Lynch's lifelong dream of becoming WWE Women's Champion happened at *Backlash 2016*. In a Six Women Elimination Match, Lynch outlasted Alexa Bliss, Naomi, Nikki Bella, Natalya and Carmella to create history. It was a long road for Lynch, but it shows you every WWE Superstar has to start somewhere to carve their road to success.

SMACKDOWN LIVE WOMEN'S CHAMPION

WRESTLEMANIA 32

53

BOBBY ROODE

HEIGHT: 6'0"
WEIGHT: 235 pounds
FROM: Toronto, Canada
SIGNATURE MOVE: Glorious DD

The Glorious One has been on a glorious streak since arriving at NXT. He defeated Shinsuke Nakamura to secure himself as NXT Champion. But the man with the It Factor has a notorious mean streak as well. He brutally defeated Tye Dillinger before his championship run. Yes, he is glorious, but Bobby Roode is definitely only interested in himself.

THE AUTHORS OF PAIN

WEIGHT: 620 pounds (combined)
Members: Akam, Rezar and Paul Ellering
SIGNATURE MOVES: The Last Chapter, Super Collider

Led by legendary manager and WWE Hall of Famer Paul Ellering, The AOP have completely dominated the NXT Tag Team division. They've toppled #DIY and The Revival and no single team has yet made an impact on the colossal duo. With Ellering being the brains behind the brawn, the AOP are destined to be an unstoppable team in WWE.

ASUKA

HEIGHT: 5'3"
FROM: Osaka, Japan
SIGNATURE MOVE: Asuka Lock

The Empress of Tomorrow is arguably the greatest female Superstar in NXT history. With a record setting title reign and (as of this printing) an undefeated streak in NXT, Asuka will be a name forever spoken as one of the greatest in women's wrestling.

ALEISTER BLACK

HEIGHT: 6'0"
WEIGHT: 205 pounds
FROM: The Lodge in Amsterdam
SIGNATURE MOVE: Black Mass

Not much is known about the ultra mysterious Aleister Black. But in the ring, Black is incredibly impactful and impressive so far in NXT. The dark Superstar has shown the WWE Universe just a few manoeuvres at Full Sail University, but it's been effective enough to result in a series of wins. It will not be long until Black becomes a top contender in NXT.

YOU ARE THE COMMISSIONER

The power is in your hands! Create your dream Raw or SmackDown Live roster. Pick and choose your Superstars, your champions, even your General Manager of the show you want to run!

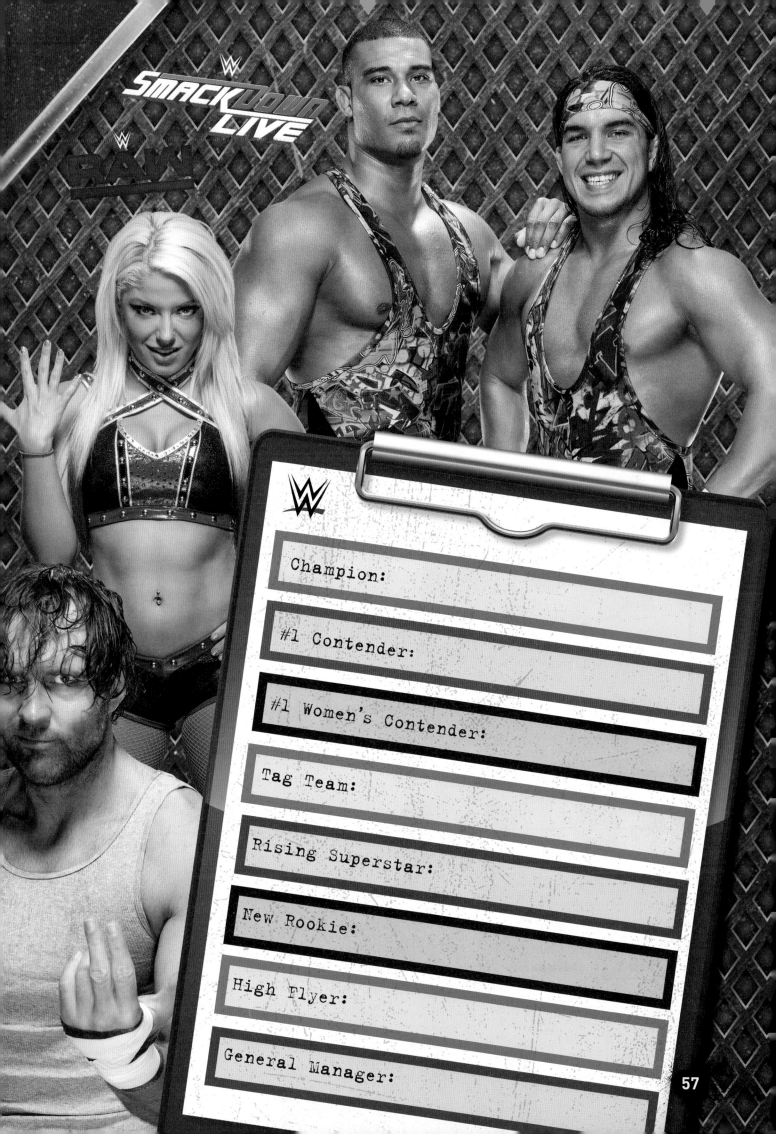

Champion:

#1 Contender:

#1 Women's Contender:

Tag Team:

Rising Superstar:

New Rookie:

High Flyer:

General Manager:

9

Times Chris Jericho has won the WWE Intercontinental Championship title. Y2J is currently the only Superstar in WWE history to win the title so many times making him, perhaps the greatest Intercontinental champion of all time.

4,830

Days spent between Goldberg's world championship reigns. When Goldberg won the WWE Universal Championship at Fastlane, it was the first time in nearly 15 years since his last title victory. That's the longest time between title reigns in WWE history.

4

Hours the cumulative time spent in the Royal Rumble by Chris Jericho. Although, he's never won a Rumble Match, Jericho has spent more time in the 30-man battle than any other Superstar in WWE history.

RECORD SETTING RECORDS

23-2

The Undertaker's incredible *WrestleMania* record. It's perhaps the only record that will remain untouched — an incredible two decade long undefeated streak at WWE's greatest show.

Alexa Bliss is currently the first and only Superstar to win both the *Raw* and *SmackDown* Women's Championship since the brand extension in 2016.

2

3

The Hardy Boys, Matt & Jeff have competed in every single *WrestleMania* tag-team ladder match. It wasn't until *WrestleMania 33*, where the Hardys won not only their first tag team ladder match at the show of shows, but they also captured the *Raw* Tag Team Championship.

In order for a Superstar to achieve a *Hall of Fame* career they must complete a series of groundbreaking WWE records. Luckily, WWE is built on a foundation of stats. It's the best way to guarantee a memorable career. Which is why records are always meant to be broken.

20

ROYAL RUMBLE

No one has ever won the Royal Rumble from the #20 position.

16

Ric Flair and John Cena are the only men in history to capture the World Championship 16 times. Triple H is close behind with 14 World Champion wins, with Randy Orton close behind with 13.

4

Times Charlotte Flair has captured the *Raw* Women's Championship. Charlotte is also the first woman to win the championship.

32

Men entered the Cruiserweight Classic in 2016. The tournament was won by TJ Perkins, the first ever Cruiserweight Champion, spawning WWE's exciting brand, *205 Live* dedicated to the Cruiserweight division.

THE BIG QUIZ

UP CLOSE AND PERSONAL!

CAN YOU FIGURE OUT WHAT'S HAPPENING WHEN THE ACTION IS THIS CLOSE? DON'T WORRY WE ADDED SOME HINTS, TO HELP DECIPHER THESE ULTRA ZOOMED IN IMAGES.

1 I'm official one-half of the Fashion Police of WWE.

2 I am the King of Strong Style.

3 This fist retired the Undertaker at *WrestleMania*.

4 This is the most exciting Championship for those who weigh under 205 pounds.

5 I'm the most dominating woman in WWE.

6 No one is more AWESOME than I am.

7 According to Chris Jericho, I'm either Todd Phillips or Mike Rome.

8 My girlfriend is the lovely, Alicia Foooooooox!

9 Without my instrument, I would truly be alone in my drifting.

10 This is my most trusted, Gentleman tool.

11 My finishing move is "No Chin Music".

12 I am the maharaja of WWE.

13 It's time to feel the glow.

14 This Raw title has only been won by a handful of Superstars and changed hands at *WrestleMania*.

15 Even with this body part injured, I still slayed the king at *WrestleMania*.

16 I am the longest reigning Women's Champion in NXT history.

17 I'd rather do everything by myself like a wolf.

18 Face the facts!

19 I am the voice of WWE.

20 When you face me, you will, go to sleep.

FIND THE ANSWERS ON PAGE 77!

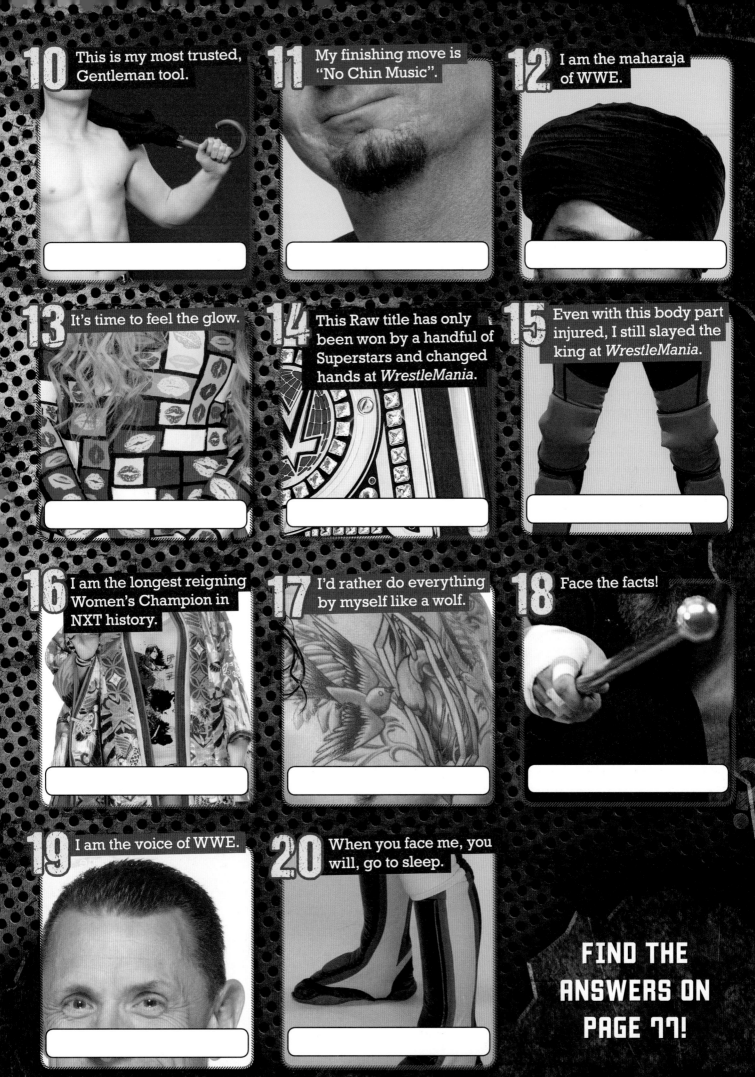

NEVILLE

HEIGHT: 5'8"
WEIGHT: 194 pounds
FROM: Newcastle, England
SIGNATURE MOVES: Red Arrow, Rings of Saturn

Although he has a bad attitude, it's hard to discount Neville's ability. The King of the Cruiserweights has ruled *205 Live* with his incredibly deep arsenal of high-flying, hard-hitting and painful submissions. Inside the ring, Neville continues to impress as he's conquered some of the best in the Cruiserweight division. It'll be hard to see if anyone can take this king off his throne.

JACK GALLAGHER

HEIGHT: 5'8"
WEIGHT: 167 pounds
FROM: Manchester, UK
SIGNATURE MOVE: Crossface Chickenwing

There is no one like Jack in all of WWE. The original Gentleman, Jack has amused WWE with his gentleman duels and not to mention the dude's got an insane mustache. But that's not to say Jack's not a serious contender. Gallagher nearly toppled the King, Neville in early-2017 with a stellar performance. But Gentleman Jack will always be a surefire, entertaining Superstar who knows how to use an umbrella in innovative ways.

RICH SWANN

HEIGHT: 5'8"
WEIGHT: 168 pounds
FROM: Baltimore, Maryland
SIGNATURE MOVE: Fantastic Voyage

Can you handle this? The fun to watch, charismatic Rich Swann has an infectious spirit. Swann can get down to boogie, but he can also get down to get the job done. Already a former Cruiserweight champ, Swann surely has his sights set on another run as Champion. Can the Superstars of *205 Live* handle another Rich Swan reign?

TJP

HEIGHT: 5'10"
WEIGHT: 175 pounds
FROM: Los Angeles
SIGNATURE MOVES: Detonation Kick, TJP Clutch

The video game character comes to life, TJP is the first ever WWE Cruiserweight Champion, winning the 32-man tournament at the Cruiserweight Classic. Since then Perkins has been near the top of the heap in 205 Live, dazzling the WWE Universe with his high flying and impactful arsenal. He's arguably the best Cruiserweight in WWE and his new, brash attitude may get him more jeers, but TJP is the kind of competitor who will do whatever it takes to win.

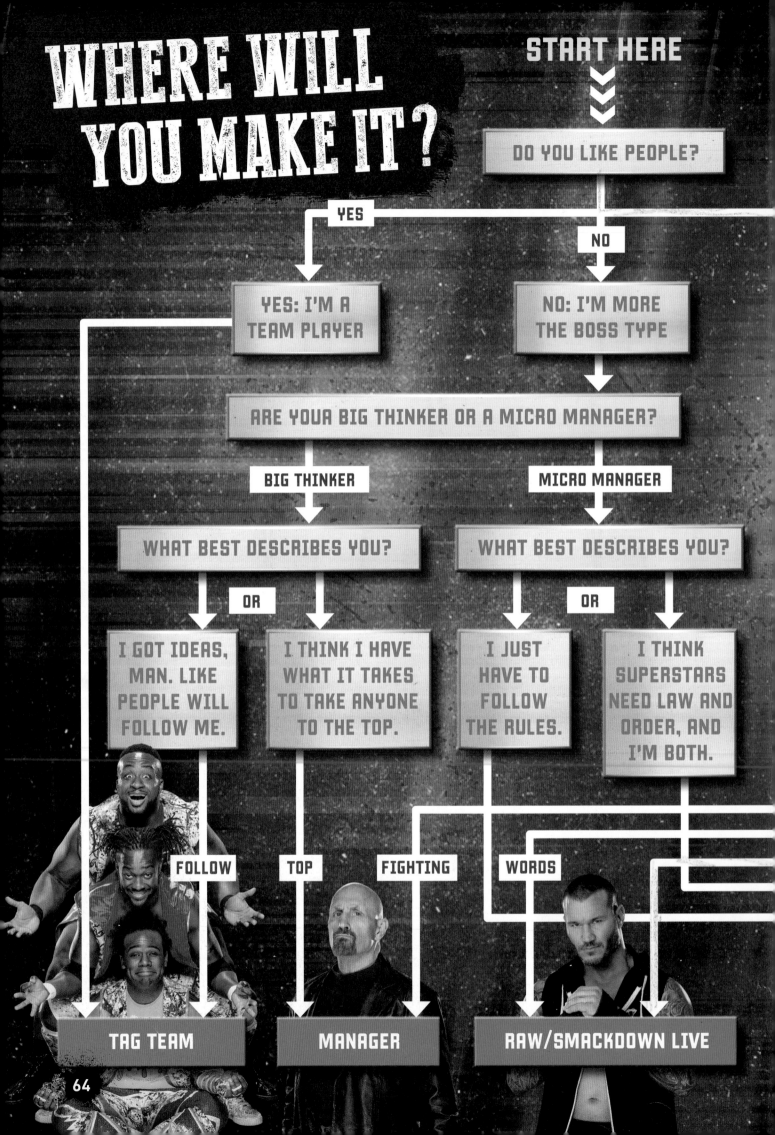

WHERE WILL YOU MAKE IT?

Members of the WWE Universe always imagine stepping into the boots of a Superstar, so here's one way to get a little bit closer. We created a flow chart to map out where you would land if you were to walk down the aisle of a WWE arena. Are you bound for cruiserweight gold, or are you heading to *Raw* or *SmackDown Live*? There's only one way to find out.

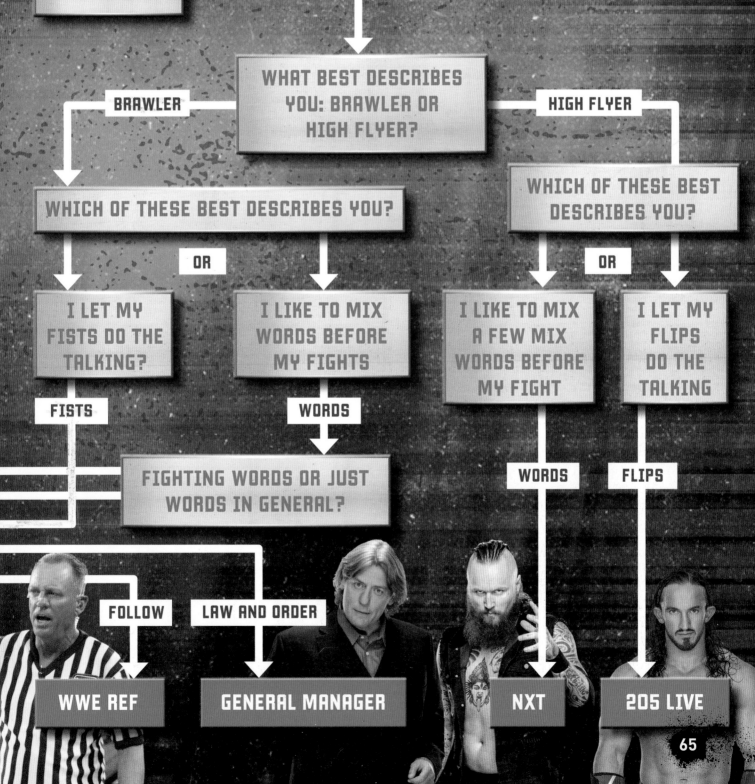

MAYBE

WHEN I NEED TO

WHAT BEST DESCRIBES YOU: BRAWLER OR HIGH FLYER?

BRAWLER

HIGH FLYER

WHICH OF THESE BEST DESCRIBES YOU?

WHICH OF THESE BEST DESCRIBES YOU?

OR

OR

I LET MY FISTS DO THE TALKING?

I LIKE TO MIX WORDS BEFORE MY FIGHTS

I LIKE TO MIX A FEW MIX WORDS BEFORE MY FIGHT

I LET MY FLIPS DO THE TALKING

FISTS

WORDS

WORDS

FLIPS

FIGHTING WORDS OR JUST WORDS IN GENERAL?

FOLLOW

LAW AND ORDER

WWE REF

GENERAL MANAGER

NXT

205 LIVE

KURT ANGLE

HEIGHT: 6'0"
WEIGHT: 220 pounds
FROM: Pittsburg, Pennsylvania
SIGNATURE MOVES: Angle Slam, Ankle Lock

In just eight years, Kurt Angle put together a WWE career for the ages. The former WWE Champion and real life Olympic gold medal winner was a milk chugging, Angle Slamming living legend. His bouts with greats like Shawn Michaels, Stone Cold Steve Austin, The Rock and Chris Jericho make him worthy of Hall of Fame status. Now, Angle is the *Raw* General Manager, a role perfect for the man of the three I's: intensity, integrity and intelligence.

BETH PHOENIX

HEIGHT: 5'7"
FROM: Buffalo, New York
SIGNATURE MOVE: Glam Slam

The historic female Superstar was one of the most dominating females inside the WWE ring. She was the second woman to enter the Royal Rumble. She's a four time Women's Champion and she even battled against Trish Stratus. Phoenix was an influential female Superstar and if she chose to, she could return to the ring today and mix it up with the current women.

SCOTT HALL

HEIGHT: 6'7"
WEIGHT: 280 pounds
FROM: Miami, Florida
SIGNATURE MOVE: Razor's Edge

"The Bad Guy" Razor Ramon, Scott Hall is one of the greatest Superstars to never win a World Championship. Despite never winning the biggest title, Hall as Ramon was one of the most influential Superstars in WWE history. He held the classic Ladder Match against Shawn Michaels at *WrestleMania X*. He's a founding member of the infamous New World Order faction in WCW and his in ring persona was one of the most memorable. When it comes to bad guys oozing machismo, there will never be anything better than Razor Ramon.

JAKE "THE SNAKE" ROBERTS

HEIGHT: 6'6"
WEIGHT: 249 pounds
FROM: Stone Mountain, Georgia
SIGNATURE MOVE: DDT

The reptile inspired Superstar legend is known for his snakes, memorable and dark charisma. But above all else, Roberts is known for creating and mastering his influential finishing move, the DDT. Roberts was a master at mind games and is known for his dark moments (like actually having one of his snakes bite Randy "Macho Man" Savage) as well as some lighter moments like teaming with rock star Alice Cooper at *WrestleMania III*. If it wasn't for Roberts' mind games, there may not be a Bray Wyatt in WWE today.

W SHOP CLASS

YOU ALREADY WEAR THE GEAR THAT DEFINES YOUR
SUPERSTAR ALLEGIANCE, BUT NOW'S YOUR CHANCE TO
MAKE THEM SUPPORT YOUR AMAZING ARTISTIC SKILLS.
THINK OF ALL OF THE ICONIC LOGOS AND IMAGES WORN
BY WWE SUPERSTARS: GOLDBERG'S TRIBAL LOGO.
THE DX LETTERS! STONE COLD'S SKULL AND AUSTIN
3:16. AND THOSE ICONIC LOGOS CONTINUE TODAY.
FROM EVERY HUSTLE, LOYALTY, RESPECT TEE
FROM JOHN CENA, THERE'S A ROMAN EMPIRE
SHIRT OR SOMETHING AS
AGGRESSIVE AS BRAUN
STROWMAN'S TEE OR
A UNICORN DESIGN
FROM THE NEW DAY.

SPOT THE NOT!

We changed ten things on these two awesome images of WWE action. Can you spot all of the slight differences? Prove you're a gold-star member of the WWE Universe by picking every single tiny altered detail on these WWE Superstars.

Check out the answers on page 77!

CROSS THE LINE

We've assembled the greatest collection of Superstar catchphrases in recent WWE memory. If you think you know your Superstars' words, then fill out the crossword puzzle. And just in case Superstar images are not enough, then use the word bank to help you slam this puzzle into oblivion.

WORD BANK

Doing	Fearless
Rocks	Double
Face	Hyped
Place	Crush
Advocate	Plan
Awesomeness	Souls
Sawft	Holes
Next	Goddess
King	Outta
Superior	Nowhere
Life	Champ
Boss	

ACROSS →

1. "How you _____?"

5. "Totally reek of _____!"

7. "You're _____!"

10. "Hug _____."

DOWN ↓

2. "Because New Day, _____!"

4. "My name is Paul Heyman and I am the _____ of Brock Lesnar."

6. "There's only one word to describe you: _____."

8. "I am the _____ of kings!"

9. "I am just genetically _____."

11. "I am the _____."

12. 'Stay _____."

13. "I'm here at the A_____ level."

14. "RUSEV, _____!!!!"

15. "I'm the man with the _____."

16. "Taking _____ and digging _____."

17 "I don't get _____. I stay _____."

ACROSS/DOWN ⇥

18. "I am the _____ of WWE."

20. "The _____ is here!"

3. "I am the _____ that runs the _____."

19. "You will get hit with an RKO _____ _____"

Answers on page 77!

73

WRESTLE-MAZE-IA

Every WWE Superstar works hard all year long to make it to *WrestleMania*. They start at *NXT*, battle through *Raw*, *SmackDown Live*, or *205 Live* and battle at countless WWE live events. Between all of the battles are their matches at pay-per-views. Can you survive the journey of a WWE Superstar in maze form? Try to battle your way through these Superstar events and end at *WrestleMania*!

START

NXT

RAW

EXTREME RULES

SmackDown LIVE

TLC
TABLES | LADDERS | CHAIRS

SUMMER SLAM

BATTLEGROUND

MONEY IN THE BANK

PAYBACK
FINISH

WrestleMania

4

Undertaker has teamed with four Superstars to win Tag Team gold: Stone Cold Steve Austin, The Rock, Big Show and his brother, Kane.

7

Undertaker has won seven World WWE Championships – including three World Heavyweight Championships and four WWE Title reigns.

23-2

The Undertaker's incredible *WrestleMania* record – 23 victories – 21 of which were consecutively known as "The Streak" and two defeats: Brock Lesnar and Roman Reigns.

2007

The year of the first and only time Undertaker won the Royal Rumble. He eliminated Shawn Michaels to win the 30-man match.

ANSWERS >> >>>

06 ODD COUPLE
1. Sheamus ⟶ Cesaro
2. Chris Jericho ⟶ The Miz
3. Goldust ⟶ Booker T
4. Mankind ⟶ The Rock
5. Daniel Bryan ⟶ Kane
6. Bret Hart ⟶ Goldberg
7. Heath Slater ⟶ Rhyno

10 SPOT THE NOT!

12 CHAMPIONSHIP SCRAMBLE

1.

2.

3.

4.

5.

6.

7.

8.

9.

10.

11.

12.

13.

16 THE BIG QUIZ
1. A	6. C	11. A	16. B
2. C	7. C	12. C	17. B
3. B	8. A	13. A	18. C
4. C	9. C	14. B	19. B
5. A	10. C	15. B	20. A

18 GIVE ME THE MIC
1. Charlotte	8. The New Day
2. Chris Jericho	9. Kevin Owens
3. James Ellsworth	10. The Miz
4. Roman Reigns	11. Bray Wyatt
5. Braun Strowman	12. Undertaker
6. Rusev	13. Bayley
7. Dean Ambrose	14. Goldberg

50 THE BIG QUIZ
1. True	6. True	11. False	16. True
2. False	7. True	12. True	17. True
3. False	8. True	13. False	18. True
4. False	9. True	14. True	19. False
5. True	10. True	15. True	20. True

60 THE BIG QUIZ

1. Fandango
2. Shinsuke Nakamura
3. Roman Reigns
4. Cruiserweight title
5. Nia Jax

6. The Miz
7. Mike Rome
8. Noam Dar
9. Elias Samson
10. Jack Gallagher

11. James Ellsworth
12. Jinder Mahal
13. Naomi
14. Universal title
15. Seth Rollins

16. Asuka
17. Baron Corbin
18. Curt Hawkins
19. Michael Cole
20. Hideo Itami

70 SPOT THE NOT!

72 CROSS THE LINE

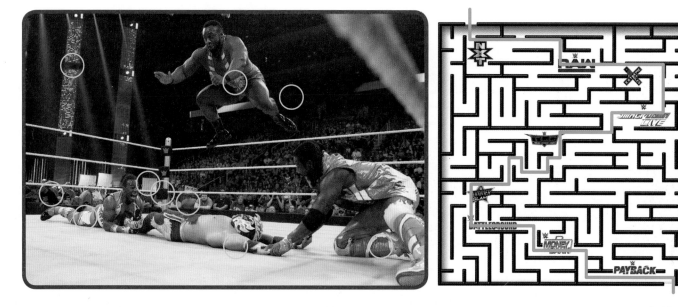

74 WRESTLE-MAZE-IA

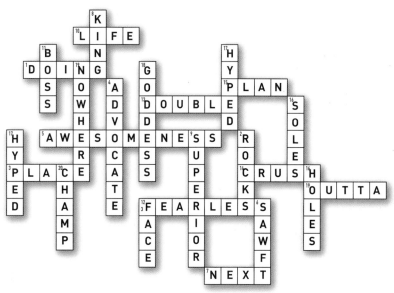